www.tredition.de

AF202353

Vanessa Maria Häufele

tears, treasures and transformation

poems for soul salvation

www.tredition.de

© 2020 Vanessa Maria Häufele

Verlag und Druck:
tredition GmbH, Halenreie 40-44, 22359 Hamburg

ISBN
Paperback: 978-3-347-21964-9
Hardcover: 978-3-347-21965-6
e-Book: 978-3-347-21966-3

SELF

A lioness, not a lamb

Gone are the days of ritual
sacrifices
And cheap compromises
Blindly giving of myself
To everybody else

Without bitterness and patiently
I now sit in the awareness of
my own
majesty
Like a lioness.

Waiting for my time to act

I took my power back

Ready to attack

And willing to protect

What is rightfully mine

Unafraid to shine

My light.

Gold is the colour of my coat

Gold is the colour of my soul

Persistence is the road

And happiness the goal.

A nomad soul

A nomad soul
Born wild and free
Forming my own destiny.

Not bound to their rules and
regulations
Authentic with my creations.
Ever-changing in my expression
With no denial or repression.

Only love and art
Inside my precious heart.

I might walk alone

But inside me I am home.

Meatsuit

This meatsuit I've been given
The one in which I am livin'
Has often felt like a prison.

But I know it serves me well
It's a tool and not a cell
It deserves my respect and care
This body my soul chose to
wear.

It deserves my loving attention
And a honorable mention
For putting up with all my shit
For all the times I tried to quit.

Hardcore idealist

I'll be a hardcore idealist
Until the day I die
There is no cure for this
I'll keep reaching for the sky.

And should I fail and all go
wrong
At least I'll know that I've been
strong
All along
And really tried my best
To find my happiness.

Artichoke heart

This is the deepest part
My artichoke heart
This is the meaty core
All that I'm asking for
All that I really need
Is to take that with me.

Remove all the layers
The thorns and the barriers
But never harm this piece
Please.

All we need

Oh, how we often move in
circles
Only ever defeating ourselves
How we often fail our purpose
By trying to be like everyone el-
se

When all we really need
Is originality
And a lot of self-belief.

Bye bye

Everything old needs to go

So that I can finally glow

Finally purified, cleansed and
freed

From all the layers of shit I've
been buried beneath.

I deserve this brand new start

I gave my all, I healed my heart

I went through this without
complaint

I always held on to my faith

When the going got real tough

I always held on to my love.

ART

An artist's plea

Refine my receptivity
Enhance my creativity
Let life flow through me
Let me be a prodigy

All I need is inspiration
Some artistic augmentation
All I need is enthusiasm
Lots of joy and lots of passion
The fuel for the implementation
Of my ideas into creations.

Simple

All I need is my loving heart
Everything else will fall into
place
All I need is to be one with my
art
So I am embraced by divine
grace.

Trust is the keyword
To some it sounds absurd
To trust with no evidence
To trust by pure reverence.

But I know this sacred path
And I know that I can last

Throught the storms and ages

I will fill all these pages

With love.

Poetry

Weigh words worthily
Arrange them into poetry
Turn them into euphony
With elegant simplicity.

Bitch, don't

Bitch don't insult my poetry

My poems are my babies

They come from deep inside of
me

They're basically a part of me.

Don't you dissect them

Inspect and correct them

Don't you analyze them

Summarize and categorize
them.

Just let them be, let them brea-
the

Revel in their idiosyncrasies

Let them leave a mark on you

Let them light a spark in you

Let them fight the dark in you

With the undeniable power of
truth.

Why I write

I don't write for success
Admiration or press
I write to heal my heart
To turn my pain into art
I write to transmute
The hurt and abuse
I write to transcend
To bend and circumvent
Societal expectations
Beliefs and limitations
Rules and regulations.

I write for peace, love, dignity
I write to set myself free.

Now my life is a work of art

Now my whole life is a work of
art
Because I follow my heart
I follow my bliss
The muses' kiss.

I do what feels right
Trust my insights
Divine inspiration
And proclamation.

I trust in the universe
Deeply immersed
In the intricate beauty

And the heavenly duty
Of life on earth.

I know my own worth.
I know my own power.
No longer a coward.

I trust in my journey
I trust in my yearning
I know I will achieve
The things in which my heart
believes.

Love is my guiding light
And happiness is my birthright.

I am free

In harmony

Nobody can take that from me.

Art is power

My art is my power

It fuels and devours
It builds up and breaks down.
All my fears are annihilated.

No security without
Following your heart's deepest
desires
No freedom without
Staying true to what you love.

This life is meant to be an ad-
venturous journey

Not a stagnant complacent pre-dicament.

It's in your hands.

Creativity

Let it stream in

Let it penetrate your core

And then pour out of your po-

res

Let it entice you

Delight and surprise you

Let it take you on a journey of

Self-discovery and love.

All too human

Too too

Too serious

Or too ridiculous

Too lazy

Or too meticulous

Too warm

Or too cold

Too timid

Or too bold

Too smart

Or too dumb

Too intense

Or too numb

Too open

Or too guarded

Too hopeful

Or too broken-hearted

Too spiritual

Or too materialistic

Too complex

Or too simplistic

Too broke

Or too rich

Trying to reach balance

can be a bitch.

So slow

I'm so very slow
That no matter where I go
in life
It takes years for me to arrive.
How did I even survive
Until now?

Streets of nothingness

I want to go home
Wherever that is
I no longer want to roam
The streets of nothingness.

I've spent quite some time there
But they don't lead anywhere
They just go on and on.

La follia

Crazy I truly am

Can't be ruled and can't be ta-
med

I am one of a kind

Out of my mind

Or maybe too deep inside?

A lunatic

A psycho-chick

Weird like the moon

Happily doomed

I dance at the brink of
nothingness

I celebrate my woman-made
mess

A female fool

I risk it all

Am I a threat to you?

Doomed

My ability to love so deeply
Will kill me in the end
I know it, I know it

My only chance to survive this
Is to forget everything
And numb myself

My love is more than anyone
can handle
Threatening
Without compromise

My love is more than I, myself,
can handle

There is no light version

It's all or nothing

So it's nothing

Cause noone wants to give their
all

Noone except me.

I still dream of complete sym-
biosis

After all these years

A love

That knows nothing but itself

That swallows everything else

Blind to the world.

Envy

Envy is an ugly trait

Much like jealousy and hate

People who can't be happy for others

Are the most crappy friends and lovers

People who hate to see you suceed

Full of bitterness and greed

They usually lack self-belief

Unsure of what they can achieve

They project their pain onto you

And want to see you small and
blue.

But don't let them get you
down
Don't you let them make you
frown
You are bigger than that
It's not worth the upset.

Learning to enjoy life again

Learning to enjoy life again
Is the hardest task I ever set out
to do
Cause after all that I've been
through
There is still some residue
Of old pain.

So close was I to giving up
Feeling stuck and out of luck
Feeling like I was born to suffer
Like life had nothing left to of-
fer.

Slowly I crawled my way back
to the light

It was one hell of a fight

Conquering the dark night

Of my soul

But now I am more whole.

Now I know more about who I
want to be

Now I know the change I want
to see

In this world

See people happy and unfurled

See everyone living their best
life

See humans thrive and not just
survive.

Patience

I have been patient all my life
waiting for something undefi-
ned.
I have always been looking out
to find out what it's all about.
I have always tried to read the
signs
and if necessary change my
mind.

Apparently it didn't work out
I'm still lost among the crowd.
I'm still as lost as I used to be
Like a boat lost at sea
floating around aimlessly.

I just got used to this state

Used to being afraid

Of doing something wrong

That will make my ordeal pro-
long.

But I don't want to live this way

I'm tired of always having to
delay

The pleasure and the joy I seek

Of always feeling mild and
meek.

I'll take a bet against the gods

That I'll make it despite all odds

That I'll succeed in my own way

and rewrite my destiny.

All bad things

Liars and snakes
Phoneys and fakes
Betrayal and deceit.

Mindgames and manipulation
Concealment and interrogation
Distrust and dishonesty.

Misfortune and pain
Struggle and strain
Heartbreak and sorrow.

Cruelty and perversion
Violence and coercion

Injustice and harm.

Loneliness and apathy
Hopelessness and lethargy
Neglect and abandonment.

Fear and insecurity
Doubt and impurity
Fogginess and confusion.

Overload and stress
Drama and mess
Addiction and disease.

Restless

This restlessness is killing me
I'm forever incomplete
Always caught up in my mind
Never really satisfied
Always looking for
Something more.

Pain

I don't mince words, I don't su-
garcoat

When I have to rinse hurts that
are about to explode

The pain has to make itself
known

The pain that has festered, the
pain that has grown

Over weeks, months, years, de-
cades, lifetimes.

A pain so pure, a pain so fine

It could make anyone weep

A pain so pristine, a pain so
deep.

I fell in love with a sociopath

I fell in love with a sociopath

Damn me for being attracted to
men like that

What is it about dangerous and
destructive men

That draws me in?

What is it about master manipu-
lators,

liars, fakers and haters

That turns me on?

There must be something sever-
ly wrong

With me

Some kind of inaedequacy

Not loving healthily.

I know I deserve better than that

I know I haven't yet met my match

In honesty and integrity.

Obscure obsessions

Obscure obsessions

Plus poisonous passions

Create crazy circumstances

And annul all alchemy.

Purgatory

Please free me from this purga-
tory
This never ending lesson
Rid me of my story
and of my obsessions.

This broken, ugly narrative
I don't want to live
through this.
Again.

I want peace of mind
And clarity at all times.

I don't want any more confusi-
on, heartbreak and sorrow

I don't want false hope for a
better tomorrow.

I don't want to be strong any-
more

I don't want to be hated, don't
want to be adored.

I just want to be

In eternal stillness

No more explosions

no more commotion.

The devil

If the devil can't free himself

He has to rot in his self-made
hell

It's not my responsibility to
help him out

Dogville

Forgiveness has to be earned
Lessons have to be learned
Morality has to be practiced
The dots have to be connected.

Don't expect blind mercy
You who tried to curse me
You who tried to break me
You who forsaked me

You who gave me nothing but
lies
and illusions

You who caused me nothing
but pain

and confusion.

Make no mistake

If I forgive, it's for my own sake

You need to heal yourself

Don't expect no help

From me

I am free.

Pretty insane

Tears of joy and sadness

Laughter of amusement and madness

Sighs of relief and sorrow

Waiting for a better tomorrow.

Life is a wild ride

But you cannot hide

It will find you wherever you go

It will force you to grow

It will make you learn your lessons

Through failure and through blessings.

We all came underprepared

That's why it sometimes feels unfair

But the truth is our souls asked for this

They wanted more than eternal bliss

They wanted to experience everything

The deepest love and suffering.

Pretty insane, if you ask me.

People are not

People are not options
Or possibilities
People are not objects
Or posessions
People are not drugs
Or substitutes
People are not hobbies
Or cheap entertainment.

Autumn Day

Fuck you Rilke

I build my home whenever I
want to

It's not too late

It's never too late

For love and belonging.

Spirituality

Mission statement

I am the protector of all things
sacred

Not giving in to confusion and
hatred

My mission is truth and clarity

Self-love and charity.

I cannot afford to be misled

Too much depends on my suc-
cess

I cannot afford to get mad

When my destiny is happiness.

I cannot let the devil win

He only ever champions sin

He only ever feasts on pain

He only ever sickens the sane.

I will hold on tight to divinity

I will hold on till infinty

I will never let my heart grow
dark

I will always keep my inner
spark.

Sometimes I feel like Joan of Arc

A woman with a vision

But will the world listen?

Will they understand the ur-
gency

Of setting ourselves free?

Will they see the necessity

Of building a new society?

Will they take her seriously

Will they follow her lead?

Or will they ridicule her

Try to belittle and fool her?

Will they secretly envy her fight

Will they be blinded by her
light?

Will they feel threatened by her
Try to sabotage and try her?
Or will they even be willed
To have her killed
To hide the truth?

I am enough

I am enough
I don't have to bluff
I don't have to pretend
To be more than I am.

Sometimes happy, sometimes
sad
Sometimes wise and sometimes
mad
Sometimes a bit complicated
That's the way I was created.

All my perfect imperfections
Have led me down my own di-
rection

And it's a journey I embrace

Learning more with each new phase.

I know the value that I hold

No matter what I have been told

The voices of those unsatisfied

Are not allowed into my mind.

As I unravel my destiny

I am protected by forces unseen

And all they ever wanted me to be

Is healthy and free.

Free to express my own truth

Feeling like I have nothing to
lose

But only to gain self-respect

For keeping my soul intact.

Be your own light

The love has to come from the
inside

Only you can make it feel right

Only you can set your heart free

Only you've got the key.

Others might praise or degrade
you

Try to deter or persuade you

But only you can set your cour-
se

Decide on shortcuts or detours.

Follow your inner knowing

Follow the signs that are sho-
wing

Trust in the universe's nudges
Let go of fears and grudges.

Life is not about struggle and
pain
Heartache and strain
It's about laughter and love
The raw expericence of
Aliveness.

Self-parenting

Be your own mom

Be your own dad

Give yourself the love you ne-
ver had

Give yourself permission to be

Heard, felt and seen.

Talk kindly to yourself

Embrace yourself with warm
and tender thoughts

Take good care of your preci-
ous body

Put yourself to bed at night

Look in the mirror and smile at
your face.

Patiently guide yourself through life's lessons.

Mourn your losses and rejoice in blessings.

Protect your dreams and aspirations

Save yourself unnecessary complications

Never give up on yourself but don't push too hard.

Try to stay open but be on your guard.

You deserve to be loved.

End the cycle

Curses passed on from genera-
tion to generation

So many lives built on shaky
foundations

So many lives lived in fear and
frustration

So many sacrifices without sal-
vation

A sad conglomeration.

We need to stop the cycle of
human suffering

We need to clear the energy
within

We need to forgive, we need to
forget

We need to move on and live without regrets.

A new era

A new chapter full of glory and
hope

No more walking a tightrope

No more fighting for survival

No more enemies and rivals

Only love and cooperation

Kind and clear communication.

All needed

We are all needed

No one lives in vain

Everyone has an important part
to play

A relevant role

In the greater whole

Don't ever forget:

Life is right in all cases

Nothing's ever wasted.

Writing

This is more than a past-time
This is the balm
for my wounded heart
My secret thought's guard
The fruit of my spiritual labour
My soul's saviour
The cure for my loneliness
The universe's sweet caress.

This is self-mastery
Dedicated yet free
Deliberate but in flow
Watching words unfold
Watching meaning grow.

This is the tool and the purpose
Independently of service.

Miracles

Miracles always come along
When you least expect them
The universe is never wrong
In how it enacts them

Only the patient and faithful are
rewarded
Not those who are doubtful
and guarded.

Be ready to be surprised and
delighted
Stay half calm and half excited
Let the universe do what it does
best

No reason to control or test.

You just have to believe

And be ready to receive.

Now

No more thinking about timeli-
nes

No more waiting for the right
time

Without a doubt:

Life is now

With or without

You.

I need to experience the mo-
ment

I am sick of ambiguous omens

I just want to be present

In touch with my essence.

Karma

Beware the ties that bind
They can mess with your mind
They can keep you stuck
They can keep you blocked.

Reenacting the same patterns
Life after life
Won't help you get better
Won't help you to thrive.

Break out of this vicious cycle
Be more than just life's disciple
Become your life's director
A conscious manifestor.

Cut

Clear as a crystal

Sharp as a scissor

I am letting go of all that do-
esn't serve me

anymore

Cutting all toxic cords

Once and for all.

There is no room for negativity

Inside of or around me

There is no room for doubt and
lack

mentality

Because I deserve to be happy.

Hibernation

In this hibernation
This phase of preparation
and recuperation
we have to keep our patience.

Let the cosmos lull you to sleep
Keep you sheltered in the deep
Keep you safe from harm
Keep you soft and warm.

Rest your pretty head
Don't look too far ahead
Relax and let go
Cause sooner than you know

The sun will shine again.

Stillness

Sometimes

when the inner turmoil gets ti-
red of itself

And the others finally leave me
alone

I can feel it.

A sense of peace and quietness,
that is so

different from what I am used
to.

My busy mind keeps pushing
me forward

And rest's a seldom thing.

My emotions still too often get
the best of me.

But in those few precious mo-
ments
where I am at one with myself
And, maybe, even the universe
I am free.

Surrender and accept

Surrender and accept
Forgive and forget
There's nothing you can do
It's the uncomfortable truth.

Don't try to comprehend
What you cannot understand
Just let this shit go.

A lyrical let-go

A lyrical let-go
A final echo
Of a love long gone.

Yes, you did me wrong
But I finally moved on
Beyond the blame and the rage
Beyond the pain and the ache.

I did so for myself
No time for self-made hells
No time for cheap distractions
I have to keep direction
Enlightenment is calling me

Telling me to set myself free.

I try my best
And know I am blessed.

Eternal evolution

Eternal evolution
There's no standing still
Each life a contribution
To a greater will.

Life is looking for itself
Through your eyes
You are here to help
The universe get wise.

You are here as a cocreator
To wake up to your true nature
And accumulate important data.

All of your experiences are stored

In a cosmic library

And you are adored

For being one of the very

Brave souls to incarnate

On earth

in this time and age.

At last

At last

All false idols are unmasked

All illusions are cleared

I faced all I feared.

It's a painful process, no de-
nying that

It makes you sad and drives you
mad

But in the end it's all worth it

When you got rid of all the
bullshit

You feel so light and free

And get to where you want to
be.

Nothing weighing you down
Noone pushing you around
Just sweet relief
And a deep-seated inner peace.

Last incarnation

Wrap it all up

Make it compact and clear-cut

Tie up loose ends

Make amends

Leave this world

With a clear conscience

And your mission accomplis-
hed.

Tarot

3 of swords

You promised me sweet sup-
port

In removing all the swords
from my heart

My pain is ancient, that much I
know

It follows me wherever I go

But I want to move through it

I want to undo it

Just give me the person I want
the most

To help me deal with all the
blows.

King of wands

You are my king of wands
The only one I really want
The only one I need
To make my dream complete.

Let me be your empress, babe
No other man can take your
place
I sit here waiting patiently
Anticipating you with me.

I will never let you down.

4 of wands

I need a stable basis

A private oasis

A place of protection

A caring connection

Someone to depend on

Someone loving and strong

To be at my best.

Love

Dragonfly

If you are a dragon

And I am a butterfly

Does that make our love a dra-
gonfly?

Will I be too gentle

Will you be too wild?

Will we have trouble to define

This bond

Will we be able to look beyond

Superficial differences?

Will we bring each other bliss?

Will we work well as a team

With our reunited stream

Of consciousness?

Or will we create a mess?

Not an option

I am not an option
I am the only one
To be cherished for a lifetime
And beyond.

Treated with the uttermost
respect
Love, kindness and tact
I deserve unwavering loyalty
I deserve passion and sensuality
I deserve to be blessed
I deserve nothing but the best.

Partners in life

Partners in life
Cause we don't do crime
Supporting each other
More than just lovers

Working together
For now and forever
A powerful team
A realized dream
A sacred union
A true communion
Infinitely blessed
With love and happiness.

An offer

I offer you my trust and loyalty

I offer you my sympathy

I offer you my time

I offer you my advice

I offer you my support

I offer you my heart

I offer you my embrace

I offer you the rest of my days

I offer you all I have to give

Will you accept this gift?

Writing, my love

My oldest passion
My long-time friend
My favourite obsession
The only one who understands.

You let me express myself
freely
You let me experience healing
You are something I can see my
worth in
You make me a better person

You are non-judgemental
Highly influential

But confidential

I don't have to share you

If I don't want to

But unlike any real lover

I can

And I want to.

That's what I want

Your wam embrace
Your infinite grace
Your tender touch
Your gentle lust
That's what I want.

Joy and pleasure
Love and leisure
Passion and affection
Comfort and connection
That's what I want.

Our spiritual ascension
Our cosmic convention

Our hearty laughter
Our happily ever after
That's what I want.

The sweetest change

You made me see the world in a
different light

Changed my ideas of wrong and
right

You made me find eternal bliss

In just one simple kiss.

With you I can finally become

The one I was meant to be all
along.

Our powers aligned

Create a synergy

That can't be denied.

You are my best friend, my lo-
ver and so much more

You opened all the right doors.

Always united in spirit and he-
art

I know we'll never be apart.

You

You are my ace of cups
You are my greatest luck
You are my firm foundation
You are my sweetest sensation

You are my rock and my wave
You keep me moving and safe
You inspire and uplift
You protect and persist.

Love is

Love is the only thing that never dies
ver dies

Love is the basis of life

Love transcends time and space

Love never goes to waste.

Love is expressed in endless
ways

Love is not something we have
to chase

Love is free and love is kind

Love transcends the human
mind.

MIX

Papier | Fördert
gute Waldnutzung

FSC® C083411

Zeitfracht Medien GmbH
Ferdinand-Jühlke-Straße 7
99095 Erfurt, Deutschland
produktsicherheit@kolibri360.de